The Light of Understanding

Franzeska G. Ewart
Illustrated by Denny Bond

Rigby®

A Harcourt Achieve Imprint

www.Rigby.com
1-800-531-5015

Literacy by Design Leveled Readers: *The Light of Understanding*

ISBN-13: 978-1-4189-3796-6
ISBN-10:   1-4189-3796-7

Printed in China
1A 2 3 4 5 6 7 8 985 13 12 11 10 09 08 07

Contents

CHAPTER 1

The Science Fair

Danny Lopez stared at a stick insect in the tank on his table. The stick insect, swaying back and forth on its pin-thin red legs, stared back at him. It looked pretty threatening, and its tank smelled awful.

"Now, class," Mr. Jackson's voice boomed from the back of the biology classroom, "raise your hand if you haven't explained to the class your project for the science fair next week."

Danny slowly raised his hand, glancing around the room at the other students. His stomach sank as no one else raised a hand. He bent over the tank, letting his straight black hair fall over his face.

Trying to hide was useless, though. He knew Mr. Jackson was looking right at him.

"Daniel Lopez," the teacher said at last. "Do you realize you are the only student who hasn't explained your project?"

As Mr. Jackson walked toward him, Danny's brain raced, searching for yet another excuse, but he couldn't think of anything. He stared miserably at the stick insect, wishing he could trade places with the bug. Surely stick insects had a much easier life than he did. They didn't have homework or teachers asking questions or a mom who was hardly ever home.

"Phew!" Mr. Jackson waved the air with one hand and held his nose with the other. "Danny, when did you last clean out your tank? Do you want to make your audience pass out at the fair next week?"

To Danny's relief, Mr. Jackson didn't seem to expect an answer. As the bell rang, the students began to gather their things together. Danny packed his notebook and textbook into his backpack, keeping one eye on the door, desperate to escape.

"Hey, we need to talk, Danny." Mr. Jackson's voice wasn't angry, however. It was soft and serious, which was worse.

The last thing Danny wanted to do was talk to anyone, but he knew that Mr. Jackson wouldn't give up. Danny had been trying to avoid Mr. Jackson for days. Now Danny couldn't escape.

"So, Danny," Mr. Jackson said as the last student left the classroom, "are you going to tell me what's wrong?"

Danny felt his cheeks redden. He didn't like it when people tried to get inside his head. His problems were no one else's business. Besides, even if he wanted to tell Mr. Jackson what was wrong, how could he ever find the words? Danny pretended to concentrate on the tank.

"Look, Danny," Mr. Jackson went on, "I know you're a bright kid. When you do your work, it's brilliant! But in the past few months, you haven't been turning in your work. Are you having trouble with what we're studying right now? Do you need help?"

The tears sprang into Danny's eyes too quickly for him to do anything about them. "My dad used to help me." His voice seemed to come from somewhere else.

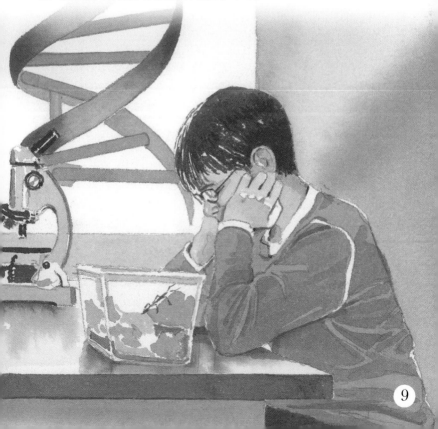

Mr. Jackson leaned forward. He bent his head to one side, trying to see into Danny's eyes. "I'm sorry, Danny. Do you want to talk about it?"

Danny shook his head and tried to hide the hot tear that was just about to roll down his cheek.

"What about your mom?" Mr. Jackson went on gently. "Can she help you?"

That did it. One tear chased another down Danny's cheeks. Like a river overflowing, all his pent-up emotion flooded out.

"The only thing my mom's got time for is her precious scientific research!" Danny exploded. "And since Dad died," he went on, more to himself now than to Mr. Jackson, "she's even busier. She's got no time for me."

After a few moments, Danny looked up at his teacher. When he did, he noticed that Mr. Jackson wasn't upset by Danny's words. And he was holding a book. Danny thought it was strange that he hadn't noticed it before. It must have been in Mr. Jackson's lab coat pocket.

Amazed at Mr. Jackson's calm reaction, Danny kept on looking at him, only now noticing the steadily growing sparkle in the teacher's kind brown eyes.

To Danny's shock, the sparkle continued to grow until it formed a silver-blue cloud around them both. The light was so bright that Danny had to screw his eyes shut, and even then he could still see it. It was as though the silvery-blue light was somehow inside of his head, behind his eyelids!

CHAPTER 2

A Strange Journey

"Open your eyes, Danny. The light won't hurt you."

As Danny opened his eyes, he felt as though his body had dissolved and every atom inside him was moving faster and faster. Then he felt as though his feet were rising off the ground.

"Hold onto this, Danny," Mr. Jackson told him, holding the leather-bound book toward him.

Danny obeyed him and touched the book. As soon as he did, the only thing he was aware of was the blue light that completely surrounded him.

At last the light began to fade and Danny's body began to feel more solid. He could feel his feet touch the earth once more, and as his head cleared, he realized he was still holding onto one corner of the book while Mr. Jackson held onto another. Danny quickly let go of the book. The teacher acted like nothing strange had happened and walked toward the door of a building that looked like an old shed. Danny was confused. Where was the biology classroom? Where was the school?

"Where are we?" Danny asked. "What just happened?"

Mr. Jackson didn't answer, but he smiled comfortingly and held up the strange book. Danny stared at the faded gold letters on its cover.

"*The Journal of Marie Curie*," he read. "Wasn't she a famous scientist?"

Mr. Jackson eased the door of the shed open and stepped inside. "You could say that, Danny. After all—she did win the Nobel Prize twice!"

Mr. Jackson shook his head in awe. "Not only did she win the Nobel Prize twice," he added, "she was the first woman ever to win it. Welcome to her lab."

Still dazed, Danny followed Mr. Jackson. As soon as he was inside the shed, harsh smoke gripped his throat while his eyes watered from the strong smell. Coughing and struggling to breathe, he looked around in horror at the shabby, dimly lit room.

Through a mist of smoke he could see wooden benches, big round bottles set in woven straw baskets, and a mass of ancient-looking instruments. All around the peeling walls glowed the ghostly shapes of bottles and tubes.

Danny's watering eyes made out the figure of a woman in a long gray dress. She was using a big metal rod to stir a vat of steaming liquid, which was the source of the harsh smoke and strong smell. Every now and then she paused to wipe a stray strand of wavy brown hair from her forehead.

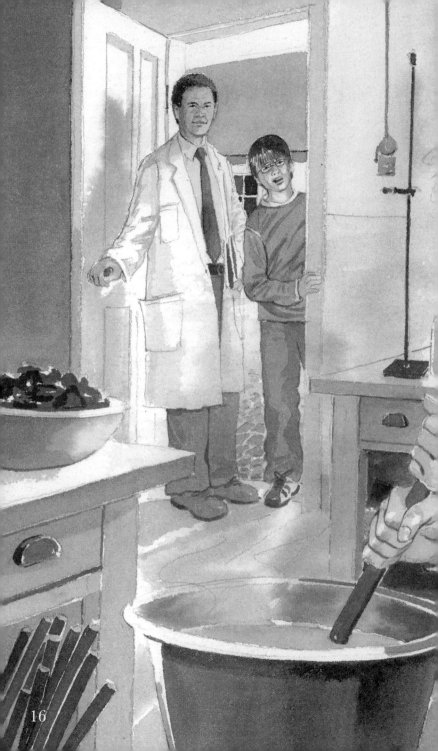

"Wow! How can anyone work here?" Danny asked, picturing his mom's bright, air-conditioned lab at the Institute of Biological Sciences.

Danny suddenly noticed how tired Marie Curie seemed. When he looked at her hands, he gasped out loud. They looked red and sore. "What's she doing?" he asked.

"She's heating up something called pitchblende," Mr. Jackson answered. "It's a mineral that can be found in some mines. She is trying to separate what it's made of so she can study it."

Danny's head buzzed with questions. "But why do it alone? Hasn't she got people to help her, like Mom does?"

Mr. Jackson didn't answer. Instead, he opened the journal and held it close to one of the glowing bottles. In the dim light Danny could just make out some scrawled handwriting. He strained his eyes to read it, but it was in a language he didn't understand.

"Do you see, Danny," Mr. Jackson said, pointing, "how there are two different kinds of handwriting?"

Danny nodded. It was clear two people had written in the book.

"Marie worked with her husband, Pierre," Mr. Jackson explained. "Together they discovered the elements they named radium and polonium. Polonium was named after Poland, the country where Marie was born. However, radium, named after the Latin for 'ray,' was Marie and Pierre's most important discovery."

Something clicked in Danny's brain then. "Radium?" he echoed. "Isn't that what they use for radiotherapy, to cure cancer?"

Mr. Jackson placed a hand on Danny's shoulder. "That's right, Danny," he said. "Radiotherapy can destroy cancer cells. Many people have been helped by radiotherapy, and many more will be helped in the future. Of course, the treatment doesn't always work," he added gently.

Danny tried very hard not to think about his dad. He and his mom had hoped so much for the radiotherapy to help his dad's cancer. But like Mr. Jackson said, it didn't always work.

Danny tried to change the subject. "So Marie worked with her husband? That must have made her life easier."

Mr. Jackson's face became solemn for a moment, but he nodded. "Look, Danny," he said, turning to another page in the journal. "This entry is in English."

> *"I had to spend a whole day mixing a boiling mass with a heavy iron rod nearly as large as myself. I would be broken with fatigue at the day's end . . ."*

Marie's words "broken with fatigue" reminded him so much of his mom—trailing home late every evening, struggling to stay awake long enough to make dinner, and then collapsing in front of the television briefly before going to bed.

Danny read on:

> *"The feeling of discouragement that sometimes came after unsuccessful toil did not last long . . . We had happy moments devoted to a quiet discussion of our work, walking around our shed."*

Danny looked back at Marie. She was struggling to move the vat off the wooden bench toward an instrument covered in dials.

"That's the Curie electrometer," Mr. Jackson explained. "Pierre invented it, and he and Marie used it to measure the radioactivity of the elements they separated out of the pitchblende."

"So she and Pierre worked together all their lives?" Danny asked.

"Yes, they worked together for many years," Mr. Jackson said, "but tragically, in 1906 Pierre was run over by a carriage and killed. From then on, Marie was on her own."

Danny felt sadness and grief twist his stomach, but Mr. Jackson went on. "Actually," he said, looking carefully at Danny, "she wasn't completely alone after Pierre died."

"How do you mean?" Danny asked, as the room filled with smoke again.

Danny could feel a tickle start in his throat. Mr. Jackson was still flipping through the journal. He didn't seem to have heard Danny. "How do you mean?" Danny asked again, a little louder this time.

Mr. Jackson steered Danny closer to the door, where the air was a little clearer. "Later, Danny," the teacher said. "I'll tell you when we're back in the classroom."

"Back?" Danny repeated, disappointed. There were still so many questions he wanted to ask! He stood beside Mr. Jackson in silence, a hundred different thoughts tumbling around inside his head.

CHAPTER 3

An Important Discovery

The smoke had started to clear again, making the lab look less shabby. Marie's face didn't seem as tired and worn, either. Despite her enormous concentration—or perhaps, thought Danny, because of it—the scientist had a deep sense of peace in her expression.

Out of the corner of his eye, Danny saw that Mr. Jackson was turning the pages of the journal. Every now and then he glanced over at Danny as if waiting patiently for him to speak. At last Danny decided what he wanted to ask. "Why?" he said. "*Why* do scientists work so hard at what they do?"

Mr. Jackson laughed. "Wow! That's some question, Danny!" But instead of answering, he said, "Why do *you* think they do it?"

Danny was used to hearing Mr. Jackson answer a question with another question. He did it all the time in biology class. Danny knew Mr. Jackson did it to make the students think, but it could be very frustrating sometimes.

This time, though, Danny thought long and hard before he answered. "I used to think Mom and Dad were scientists because of the money," he said slowly. "After all, isn't that why most people work hard?"

Mr. Jackson looked like he wanted to laugh again. "Marie certainly wouldn't agree with you there, Danny," he said. "She and Pierre always struggled to make enough money. As for Marie's early days in Paris," Mr. Jackson went on, "she lived in a garret—a tiny attic room—that was small and cramped. She often had too little to eat and hardly enough coal to use in the fireplace to warm herself. The water she used to wash with would often freeze on winter nights!"

"So what kept her going?" Danny asked, hardly able to believe how difficult life must have been for scientists like Marie Curie.

In answer, Mr. Jackson pointed to a passage in the journal that read:

"All that I saw and learned that was new delighted me. It was like a new world opened to me, the world of science . . ."

Danny looked back at Marie. She was holding up a glowing tube, closely examining its contents. Danny felt it was remarkable that, as exhausted as she was, Marie's eyes still sparkled.

"Surely," he thought, "there must be times in Mom's lab when she discovers something new. Maybe at those times her eyes sparkle like that."

"So, is that why scientists work so hard?" he said at last. "Because of the thrill of finding out something new?"

Mr. Jackson nodded. "Yes, Danny," he said. "That's part of it. Scientists want to know how things work. If they know how things work, they've got a better chance of fixing them when they go wrong."

The teacher's brown eyes pierced through the gloom of the shed like a laser, and Danny blinked and stared hard, realizing that something strange was happening again. This time, however, he knew that the light was growing into a cloud that would soon surround them both. Time, Danny knew, was running out. And suddenly things began to fall into place.

"It's about finding the *truth*, isn't it?" Danny said, his words tumbling out excitedly. "It's about searching and searching and finally being sure you've got the right answer!"

"Exactly, Danny," nodded Mr. Jackson. "Often, we're in the dark about things. We just can't see clearly–"

"Then, when we *do*," Danny interrupted, "we say we've seen the light!"

"Let me tell you one last thing Marie wrote," Mr. Jackson said. "It's another very important reason why dedicated scientists work so hard."

Danny could barely feel the floor beneath his feet, but they hadn't left Marie Curie's shed. Danny still didn't want to go. Not yet.

"Listen, Danny." Mr. Jackson's voice echoed in his ears, and Danny listened hard. Mr. Jackson's voice faded, and a woman's voice–Marie's voice–was speaking to Danny.

> *"You cannot hope to build a better world without improving the individuals . . . Our particular duty . . ."*

But her voice faded before Danny could hear all of what she had to say. Desperate to know what that "particular duty" was, Danny concentrated hard on what Marie's shed looked like. He could feel the floorboards once again under his feet, and the brilliant blue light faded enough for him to see Marie for what he knew would be the last time.

She was so near, he could have touched her. Her head was bent, and when Danny looked down he saw she was writing in a journal that looked exactly like the one Mr. Jackson was holding in his hand. With a shock, Danny realized it was the same journal.

Danny peered through the dim light, hardly daring to breathe, watching the letters form. The language was strange to him, but in that amazing moment he knew what the words said.

"Our particular duty . . ."

the sentence began. On and on Marie wrote and as she did, Danny read the words out loud, wanting to understand everything:

". . . is to aid those to whom we think we can be most useful."

At that moment Marie looked up at Danny. Wordlessly, they stared into one another's eyes across the decades of time that separated them.

"Danny," Mr. Jackson's voice broke the moment. He held Marie's journal out toward Danny. "We have to go back now," he said.

Mr. Jackson gently shut Marie's journal. As Danny touched the book, the light once again became blinding. The last thing Danny saw before he felt as though his body dissolved was the hint of a smile on Marie Curie's face.

CHAPTER 4

Danny's Surprise

The house was dark and silent when Danny arrived home, and for once he was glad. He needed time alone after all that he'd been through that afternoon.

He dumped the smelly insect tank on the kitchen counter and began to fish out the moldy leaves, carefully shaking the stick insects into a bowl. As he did, they snapped their legs together like soldiers and lay stick-still.

Fascinated, Danny watched as the stick insects decided to come back to life. Cautiously, they began to sway like plants in a breeze. Danny felt bad that he hadn't cleaned out their tank for so long.

He got some newspaper, tipped over the tank, and, trying hard not to breathe in, scraped out the mess sticking to the bottom of the tank. He was about to toss the dirty newspaper into the garbage can when he noticed something. He blinked, looked again, and laughed out loud in surprise and delight.

The newspaper was crawling with life! What he had thought was just a bunch of rotting leaves was actually a swarm of baby stick insects, each one an exact, tiny copy of its parents.

"How in the world," Danny thought, "could these little creatures possibly grow into adults?" Their legs were like wood splinters–they looked too brittle to allow for growth.

But somehow they did grow up. Amazed, Danny stared at the tiny creatures while an idea formed in the back of his mind. Maybe his science fair presentation could be about how the baby stick insects grew up into adult stick insects.

His thoughts were interrupted by the clock in the hall chiming five, reminding him that he was hungry. He washed and dried the tank, layered the bottom with more leaves from the garden, and carefully transferred the insect family to their much improved home.

Normally at five o'clock, Danny would eat some cheese and crackers while he watched television and waited for Mom to get home and make dinner.

Today, however, the events of the afternoon came flooding back. He could almost smell the smoke of Marie Curie's lab again and he remembered, as clear as day, everything Mr. Jackson had shown him in her journal. Most of all, though, he remembered the very last question Mr. Jackson had answered, the one he had refused to answer in the shed.

Back in the biology classroom, Danny had asked him again, "So, why wasn't Marie Curie completely alone after Pierre died?" Mr. Jackson had given him that same piercing look before telling him.

"She had her daughter, Irène," he had said at last. "Irène worked side-by-side with Marie, and during World War I, they used their radium tubes to help injured soldiers. Irène became a famous scientist as well, and she and her husband won the Nobel Prize in 1934."

Danny had said nothing. He had gathered up his backpack and the stick insect tank and had muttered a rather embarrassed "thank you" before shuffling his way out of the classroom. Mr. Jackson had followed him, managing to catch Danny's backpack just in time as he dropped it in the doorway.

Danny had thought at the time that it had taken Mr. Jackson a little too long to return the backpack. He had seemed to be fumbling about with the buckles.

Now Danny opened the kitchen cupboard and took out a loaf of bread to make some sandwiches. By the time Mom staggered in, her arms full of grocery bags and papers from work, the table was set, the milk was poured, and their dinner was ready.

Mom nearly dropped her grocery bags. "Danny!" she beamed. "You are wonderful! This meal looks delicious."

Danny beamed back and sat down, ready to eat.

As they cleaned up the kitchen together after the meal, Danny told his mom about his discovery in the insect tank.

"I thought it was just a great big mess at the bottom of the tank," he told his mom excitedly, "and I nearly threw them in the garbage! But how do they grow, Mom? How can their legs get bigger when they're so hard?"

"Whoa! Hang on, Danny!" laughed Mom. "It's a lot to explain! Let's go to my office, and I'll show you some pictures on the Internet."

In her office, Mom quickly started up her computer. "First of all Danny, you have to understand the idea of the insect exoskeleton," she explained. "An exoskeleton, which is what the hard shell of the insect's body is called, supports and protects the insect's body like armor. Is this for your science fair next week?"

Danny nodded his head. "Yes, it is." He hesitated a second, then said, "I was wondering if you could help me put together my presentation for the science fair. I don't even have a title yet, and I need to explain my project in class tomorrow."

Danny waited for his mom to say she was too busy. He waited for her to say, "Maybe tomorrow, Danny. I'm too tired right now." But that's not what she said.

"I'd be happy to, Danny," Mom said.

All that evening, Danny's mom told him about the stick insect life cycle. She explained how an insect molted, or shed its hard exoskeleton in order to grow a new, larger exoskeleton.

She told him how different chemicals in the insect's body caused these changes to take place, and slowly Danny began to understand.

That evening Danny felt the first real thrill of discovery, like what he imagined his mom must feel sometimes in her lab. He decided to ask her about her research.

"I'm trying to understand more about transplants, Danny," she told him. "We can do so much now—give people new hearts, new kidneys, even new faces! But there can still be problems if someone's body can't accept the new organ and rejects it."

Danny thought about this for a moment and then asked, "Does that happen a lot?"

His mom smiled sadly and said, "Yes, it does."

She continued, "People often have to take drugs with unpleasant side effects to help their bodies accept the new organs. I'm working on a way to help people with transplants avoid having to use those harmful drugs."

She sighed. "Sometimes I feel I'm getting nowhere, you know. And then, all of a sudden I make a discovery and it gives me new hope." She handed Danny his science fair presentation printouts. Then she closed down the computer. "Time for bed, Danny," she said, patting him on the back.

"It's been great to share all this with you," Mom said. "We've not spent enough time together since Dad died. I'm sorry, Danny."

As they left the office, Mom smiled a little sadly. "Work's been so difficult without him," she went on, "but however discouraged I get, I always know he'd want me to keep going. It's as though we're still working together. And I know we have an important purpose."

She paused for a moment and then hugged Danny tightly. "But, Danny, you are the most important thing in my life," she finished quietly. "From now on, we'll spend more time together."

As he went into his room, Danny could have sworn he heard a soft voice whisper in his ear:

"To aid those to whom we think we can be most useful."

On an impulse, Danny turned and faced his mom.

"Mom," he said, "would you come to the science fair and tell everyone about your work? I think if more people understood what you did, they'd see what an important job you do."

He looked at his mom, suddenly feeling awkward. But he could see from the sparkle in her eyes that the answer was "yes."

Alone in his room, Danny opened his backpack to put away his "Stick Insect Life Cycle" presentation. When he looked inside, he realized why Mr. Jackson had taken so long to hand him his backpack. Tucked in between his notebook and textbook was a small leather-bound journal. Danny hesitantly touched the corner of the journal, both afraid and excited.

Nothing happened—no blinding blue light, no floating feeling. Danny took the journal out and ran his finger once more over the faded gold letters on its cover, re-reading the magical words: *The Journal of Marie Curie.*

Danny could hear his mom in the shower, so he tiptoed along the hallway to her room, where he laid the journal on her pillow.
He hoped it would be as amazing and life-changing for her as it had been for him.